A MINIATURE
OF MUS

CW00422406

50p

A MINIATURE HISTORY
OF MUSIC

FOR THE GENERAL READER
AND THE STUDENT

BY

PERCY A. SCHOLES

M.A., D.LITT., HON. D.MUS., OXON.
HON. D.LITT., LEEDS; DR ÈS LETTRES, LAUSANNE
F.S.A., F.R.HIST.S.

FOURTH EDITION

LONDON
OXFORD UNIVERSITY PRESS

Oxford University Press, Ely House, London W. 1

GLASGOW   NEW YORK   TORONTO   MELBOURNE   WELLINGTON
CAPE TOWN   IBADAN   NAIROBI   DAR ES SALAAM   LUSAKA   ADDIS ABABA
DELHI   BOMBAY   CALCUTTA   MADRAS   KARACHI   LAHORE   DACCA
KUALA LUMPUR   SINGAPORE   HONG KONG   TOKYO

ISBN 0 19 316110 9

First published 1928
Fourth Edition 1955
Reprinted 1957, 1962, 1966, 1972, and 1974

*All rights reserved. No part of this publication may be
reproduced, stored in a retrieval system, or transmitted,
in any form or by any means, electronic, mechanical,
photocopying, recording, or otherwise, without the prior
permission of Oxford University Press*

*This book is sold subject to the condition that it shall not,
by way of trade or otherwise, be lent, re-sold, hired out, or
otherwise circulated without the publisher's prior consent
in any form of binding or cover other than that in which
it is published and without a similar condition including
this condition being imposed on the subsequent purchaser*

*Printed in Great Britain
at the University Press, Oxford
by Vivian Ridler
Printer to the University*

EXPLANATORY

The Miniature History of Music first appeared as a series of seven articles in *The Radio Times*, with the following Introduction by the Editor:

'There have been many histories of music, from the great works in several volumes down to smaller handbooks of a hundred pages or so. But here is a history which is thought to be shorter than any yet written. It consists of seven chapters, comprising about 15,000 words. It is "complete", in that it covers the ground; yet readable, in that it omits, as far as possible, all unnecessary names, dates, and facts. The series of seven chapters, while enabling the listener to "place" the various composers and styles of music included in the B.B.C.'s programmes, constitutes an easy introduction to the subject for those who wish to pursue it further in such larger treatments as the author's own *Listener's History of Music*.

CONTENTS

I. AN INTRODUCTORY CHAPTER

THE real purpose of history is to explain the present—to show how *we and our ways* came about, and thus partially to interpret us to ourselves.

This being so, it has occasionally been suggested that the proper way to write history would be to write it backwards. Mr. G. K. Chesterton, for instance, once proposed that somebody should write a History of England beginning with the 'policeman in the next street' and working back to Magna Charta. It is an interesting suggestion—but difficult! Mr. Chesterton's own History of England does not follow his ingenious plan, and my History of Music will not do so. But this much of Mr. Chesterton's idea I will accept—I will begin with 'the policeman in the next street', take a look at him, then jump back to Magna Charta, and thence push forward until I reach the policeman again.

Let us consider some world-famous conductor with his baton marshalling the orchestral traffic, keeping people out of one another's way, and controlling behaviour, as music's typical 'policeman in the next street'.

And, especially, let us intelligently examine the state of the traffic our policeman is directing. There pass before him not one crowd, but many kinds of crowds. At one moment he is admonishing a seventeenth-century London crowd who, moving to a Purcell dance-rhythm, have suddenly appeared from nowhere. At another moment he may be called on to marshal an eighteenth-century German crowd clustering around a bewigged old church musician called Bach. Then he is pleasantly

9

busied with helping on their way a group of later eighteenth-century symphonic courtiers, whose leader he addresses as Haydn or Mozart. And anon there flocks before him a rather more turbulent body of nineteenth-century Germans, following a Beethoven or a Wagner. Now and again he has to handle a procession of actual revolutionaries, crying 'Excelsior' as they rush the steps of a concert hall, and carrying a red 'banner with a strange device'—'STRAVINSKY' or 'SCHÖNBERG' or 'BARTÓK'.

Our interest aroused by our observation of the duties and position of our constable conductor, we shall visit all these peoples in their own countries and their own centuries. For the moment let us look a little curiously at only one of them—that of our own days. The Bach crowd belong to the days of our ancestors, the Bartók crowd perhaps belong to those of our descendants. Both are a little strange to us. With the Wagner crowd we all feel quite at ease. They belong to *us*; they represent the thoughts and feelings most general in musical circles (i.e. the *wider* musical circles)in our own times. I propose, therefore, first to study them, and then to do my jumping backward and working forward again.

A metaphor may become a burden or a bore. This one is now both. And so I drop it and bluntly ask the question—What are the characteristics of *normal* music of to-day? And by 'normal' music of to-day I am compelled by the rather conservative instincts of our race to imply the music that came new to earth in our grandfathers' time, the age of Wagner. If we get clearly into our minds these characteristics we shall be the more interested in seeing how they have originated and where they have come from.

The first thing that strikes us about a Wagner piece is its use of a large orchestra. We see, massed up there on the platform, a huge body of string players and considerable bodies of wind and percussion players. At times one of these bodies, as a whole, takes the predominant place in the pleasant assault on our ears. At other times a single group, like the First Violins, or a single instrument, like a Horn or Clarinet, may do so. But whatever the predominance of the one instrument, or the one group, the other members of the orchestral force have usually got something valuable to do. Listening carefully we find that even when one member of the orchestra is made to 'stand out', the others (or many of them) are usefully and interestingly employed. Not one melody only is going forward, but several, woven together into a marvellously coloured musical web.

That element we call COUNTERPOINT—the placing of points or notes counter to or against one another so that they form melodies, each melody beautiful in itself and the whole fitting beautifully together.

The elements of variety of 'colour' and of 'weaving' (or of ORCHESTRATION and Counterpoint) are, then, obviously two very essential elements in the music of Wagner and his day.

Another point that must strike us is the mastery with which the notes combined at any given moment merge to make a glowing or a sombre mass. There seems no end to the variety of effect produced by these note combinations or chords, the art of using which adroitly we call HARMONY. Not only, then, are vivid Orchestration and bold yet neat 'Counterpoint' characteristic of Wagner, but also subtle 'Harmony'.

Then, if we listen keenly and use both our observation

and our memory, we may note the masterly way in which tunes appear and disappear and reappear, so that we never get too much of one tune at a time, which would bore us, nor do we get too incessant a change of tune, which would constitute a severe strain on our attention. (Wagner's tunes are usually quite short, and they are called 'motifs'.) The element of variety of tune-material, and its reappearance in different guises and in different keys, is the element of FORM in music.

We have now four elements clear in our minds—Orchestration, Counterpoint, Harmony, and Form, to quote them in the rather illogical order in which they have happened to strike us as we listened to, say, the Overture to *The Mastersingers*.

The study of the growth of skill in handling those four elements is a great part of the study of the History of Music.

But Wagner's mastery of any one of these, or all four, is only a means to an end—the expression of beauty and of emotion; and as we study the music of the ages before Wagner it will be a chief interest with us to note how those elements are applied to this great end—an end which the poet attains by the use of words, the painter by the use of lines and colours, the sculptor by the use of masses, and the composer by the use of tones.

II. MUSIC AS WOVEN TONE

THE evolution of music is one of the most curious things in the world. It seems to be so rapid and so recent! For by music we to-day almost take it for granted that we mean what in the first chapter I called 'Woven Tone'. Even in a simple hymn-tune there are four 'parts' singing four tunes—soprano, contralto, tenor, and bass. The tunes may sometimes be poorish ones, but they are at least tunes in this sense, that each differs from all the rest, having more or less of its own shape and individuality.

That is, however, quite a latter-day conception of music. The Egyptians who built the pyramids, and the Greeks who left us beautiful statuary and a magnificent literature, and the Hebrew poet and prophet race all had music and all loved it, but it was (so far as we can with any certainty trace) merely *unisonal*. In the choir of Solomon's temple or the chorus of a play of Aeschylus all the participants sang the same tune.

Music as *we* know it dates back only about 1,000 years. And it took nearly 500 of those 1,000 years to make experiments which should bring about a result really justifying the conception. Moreover, to this day only European races (and to a small extent races that have come under their tutelage) sing or play in anything but unison. The others have as yet hardly begun their experiments.

What a youthful thing music is! Four or five hundred years' growth—and already some people wish to step in with a 'Thus far shalt thou go and no farther!'

The first step beyond unisonous singing was parallel

singing. Put your little finger and thumb five notes apart on the piano and play any tune in parallel lines, and you will get the idea of the singing of a ninth-century two-part choir. To turn it into a full four-part choir do the same thing with the two hands simultaneously. Now you have it!

Probably the invention of this method had a practical basis: the voices of tenors are roughly five notes above those of basses, and the voices of sopranos roughly five notes above those of altos.

As you played the tune in the way suggested, you disliked it; and if you were to go on long enough, the next-door neighbour would at last politely tap on the wall. That is, perhaps, because you and your neighbour hear the effect in the wrong way. Our modern ears are more or less trained to follow the movement of parts, and we feel that parallel fifths are, from some acoustical characteristic, rather offensive.

The seventh-century churchman, hearing plain-song treated in that way, probably heard the two parts as one; he heard the main tune (or *Cantus firmus*) thickened with a stroke of colour along its whole length. We now need to regain this knack, for modern composers (Vaughan Williams is one example) have fallen into the habit of thickening many of their 'parts' in just this way, though they usually somewhat cover the device with a clothing of real harmony in the other parts.

After a time a fresh kind of parallelism was introduced —that of three or six notes apart (much sweeter to our ears; try this also on the piano!)—and also an abandonment of parallelism, in a rough kind of constant variation of the intervals at which the accompanying voices were singing. Every stage in this progress was violently

opposed as 'modern' and outrageous, but the stages suc-
ceeded one another nevertheless. No Canute or Mrs.
Partington can control the tonal tides, which, contemptu-
ously ignoring all bulwarks erected against them, sweep
relentlessly forward according to some strange natural
law of their own.

The culmination of all this experimentation came in
the sixteenth century, when composers had learned, skilfully and with the most delicate subtlety, to adjust the
movements of their 'parts' in relation to one another.
When you hear a Mass of Palestrina or a madrigal of
Byrd you are enjoying the fine flower of a process of horti-
culture that began when, in the ninth century, some
ingenious musician first grafted distinct parts for other
voices on to the tenor plain-song ('tenor', the *holding*
part, the one that maintains the original chant).

Now Palestrina and Byrd and their contemporaries are,
practically speaking, the earliest group of composers
whose music has enough interest for the ears of to-day
ever to be broadcast or recorded for gramophone—to
take the most obvious test of popularity. Let us consider
what are some of the musical characteristics of their
choral music. We will take a Byrd Mass or madrigal as
an example.

First of all we note that the four (or three or five or six)
voices move very freely; centuries of steady experiment
have conferred on composers the necessary technique,
and they are able to set on paper a composition in which
every voice has something good and independent to sing,
whilst the successions of note combinations (or 'chords'
or 'harmonies'), induced by the meeting of the parts, are
beautiful and expressive in themselves. In this we are
already on the way to Wagner.

15

Secondly, there strikes us the frequent device of one voice entering with a little snatch of tune and another one then taking it up and singing it in overlap—a feature that adds a considerable measure of interest both for singers and hearers.

Thirdly, we observe as we listen to one piece of choral music after another that they are sung without accompaniment. They are purely choral compositions, not choral-instrumental. Such was the general custom of the day—on the whole the best day choral music has ever known.

That will be enough for us to notice on a first occasion. We have now made an intelligent acquaintance with the choral music of the kind Queen Elizabeth and William Shakespeare loved, and the kind Drake's men sang on their voyages (for we have record of their musicianship —it was a very musical age). When we hear the solo songs of the period we find them to be simple lyrical settings of fine poetry, with a deftly-made, if simple, accompaniment for the lute.

Let us now move forward through the following century.

About the year 1600 a new conception came about— *dramatic music*, in which the voice should carry out a sort of natural declamation much like that of impassioned speech. It was of this RECITATIVE, as it is called (an Italian invention), that the first operas and oratorios were largely made up. Set tunes, or airs, were, however, also soon introduced, and so were choruses. The accompaniment of the recitative was given to some instrument or combination of instruments, and was largely carried out as a succession of mere supporting chords. Here was a new aspect of music—a succession of chords frankly treated *as* chords and not brought into existence as the by-product of combinations of intertwining melodies.

This is the conception of 'Harmony' as distinct from 'Counterpoint', and it influenced all music. The chorus in operas or oratorios sometimes moved in plain blocks of harmony, or chords, the separate voice parts often having little independent melodic interest. Harmony *as* harmony began to be more studied, and with this deeper study changes took place in the ideas as to what chords could well succeed one another and also as to what scales could well be used as the raw material of music.

As to these scales, run your fingers up the white notes of the piano from D to D and you have an idea of the general flavour of just one of the large number of old scales or 'modes'. Now get your youngest girl to play you the scales of (say) D major and D minor and you have the flavour of the only two modes which retained popularity under the new harmonic conditions. That difference of 'flavour' you have just experienced is one difference you feel when you pass from a work of Byrd to a work of Bach.

Bach and his contemporary, Handel (both German by birth), Scarlatti (the Italian), and Couperin (the Frenchman) are pre-eminent representatives of the next great moment in the development of music. Music has now been worked at as both 'counterpoint' and 'harmony', and during the first half of the eighteenth century has come to a balance between these two interests, consciously recognizing the claims of both. Any chorus from Bach's *St. Matthew Passion* or from Handel's *Messiah* exemplifies this balance.

And those great works represent a century and more of development in the form of the oratorio, which still retains the recitative method of carrying forward the narrative.

It is curious that at this period the art of unaccompanied choral singing, so wonderfully cultivated earlier, has fallen into some neglect. Bach has a few (very fine) unaccompanied choral works, but Handel none.[1]

The orchestra used by Bach and Handel and their contemporaries is, as it seems to us to-day, primitive. Its basis is a keyboard instrument (harpsichord or organ), played from what is called a FIGURED BASS, i.e. the bass part of the music with a line of figures above or below it, representing the harmonies out of which the player, guided by his personal taste and skill, is to erect a more or less elaborate accompaniment.

The very existence of such a feature calls our attention to two characteristics of the musical thought of the day: first, the thorough acceptance and complete organization of the harmonic conception, which has actually found expression in a kind of shorthand; and, second, the easygoing attitude towards orchestral tone, which goes so far as to leave one of the chief performers to extemporize the details of his music.

This chapter has treated of two distinct periods, which we will for convenience call the Byrd period and the Bach period. They are both periods of *woven* music, both 'contrapuntal' periods, but with a harmonic evolution leading from one to the other and making the music of the second very different from that of the first. In *feeling* the music of the two is distinct. It is always difficult to describe 'feelings', and the best thing is to say—

[1] Even those of Bach, though they possess no independent accompaniment, are thought by some authorities to have been sung with the vocal parts doubled by the organ.

*Hear a Byrd madrigal and a Bach or Handel chorus and
'get' the difference for yourselves.*

And now for the principal (and serious) omissions of
the chapter—pure Instrumental Music and Opera. The
Instrumental Music of the period will be dealt with con-
veniently as a prelude to the next chapter, which is to be
entitled *Sonatas and Symphonies*. And more will be said
about Opera in the prelude to Chapter V, which is to be
entitled *Music as Drama*.

KEY DATES

I. THE GOLDEN AGE OF UNACCOMPANIED CHORAL
MUSIC. (Contrapuntal or 'woven' music.)

Palestrina (Italian)   *c.* 1525–94.
Byrd (English)   *c.* 1543–1623.

II. THE BEGINNING OF DRAMATIC MUSIC. (Operas and
Oratorios, with the new Harmonic Style and with
'Recitative'.)

Monteverdi (Italian)   1567–1643.

III. THE AGE OF THE BALANCE BETWEEN HARMONY AND
COUNTERPOINT.

Purcell (English)   1658–95.
Bach (German)   1685–1750.
Handel (German; naturalized British)   1685–1750

III. SONATAS AND SYMPHONIES

The Human Voice being the most natural musical instrument, its artistic use was the earliest to develop. But artificial musical instruments have existed as far back as history takes us, and must, for that matter, have existed in simple forms from remote prehistoric times.

By the date when the art of combining voices and weaving melodies had come into existence and been brought to perfection (i.e. the sixteenth century) many instruments—string, wind, and percussion—had reached a very considerable degree of perfection.

To take one example—in Queen Elizabeth's day the Viols (precursors of the Violin family, which was to become popular a century later) were very efficient and capable of being combined into groups, something like our modern String Quartet. Also there were instruments very like our modern piano in miniature, and in particular the Virginals, an early form of Harpsichord, with strings and keys like a piano, but with a plucking action instead of a hammering one.

What was as yet not much realized was the (to us obvious) fact that instruments call for a different treatment from voices, and that each type of instrument calls for a treatment different from that of every other type of instrument. Composers were, however, awaking to specifically instrumental capabilities, and the England of Elizabeth, which produced such a wonderful body of lyrical and dramatic poetry and choral song, produced also a body of fine instrumental music, and especially of keyboard music.

The same men who wrote the English madrigals and

unaccompanied choral church music produced also a mass of keyboard music that is now recognized as being the very foundation upon which the later structures of Bach, Mozart, and Beethoven are built.

Sometimes they would make a keyboard piece in this way—they would take some popular song tune of the day and rewrite it in a number of different styles, a string of versions of the original, exploiting the resources available for two hands at a keyboard. Thus doing, they were evolving that very VARIATIONS form which, in a more elaborate and expressive treatment, is found in many great pieces of Beethoven, Brahms, and almost every instrumental composer of note who has since lived.

Another form that pleased them was that of two dances in succession, two contrasted dances, a slowish Pavan and a brisk Galliard. Out of this evolved the SUITE OF PIECES, as we find it a century and a quarter later in Bach and Handel, in which five or six such dance measures follow one another, making up a set of contrasted pieces.

Still another form was the FANTASIA, a sort of keyboard madrigal, contrapuntal in style and with a good deal of that tossing of a little tune, or subject, from one 'voice' or 'part' to another that was described in the previous chapter in discussing the madrigal. Later Handel and (especially) Bach were to use this form very effectively, developed into the FUGUE—which Bach was to carry to the highest point of perfection it has ever reached or could possibly reach. From the middle of the sixteenth century to the middle of the eighteenth we see a really wonderful progress in keyboard music—a passage from the merely rudimentary to the highly developed.

Now, in any instrumental piece of length there is the problem of how to maintain the listener's interest. There are two chief means of doing this—variety of key and variety of musical material. By Bach's time the technique of using these resources had become a very subtle thing. The dance forms still remained, but they tended to disappear: there are dance forms still in Bach's many suites for keyboard and for orchestra, but it would often be difficult to dance to them. Instrumental music is steadily becoming more abstract.

And as it does so it ceases to be 'Suite' and becomes SONATA (or 'Symphony' or 'String Quartet' or 'Concerto' —all much the same type of piece, all Sonatas, so to speak, but for different media; the Sonata proper for one instrument or two, the String Quartet for four stringed instruments, the Symphony for full Orchestra, and the Concerto for one or more solo instruments with Orchestra).

With Haydn and Mozart this Sonata-Quartet-Symphony-Concerto form has become almost stereotyped. There are three or four 'movements', or pieces, including generally a quickish and longish first movement and a quickish and longish last movement, and a slow, expressive middle movement. The only definite dance relic from the Suite is the often-present Minuet.

With these composers the Sonata type of piece was often lovely and often highly enjoyable, and as they grew in experience and intellectual maturity it tended to become more emotionally expressive. Then came Beethoven, who, a deeper-feeling man than they, and the inheritor of the technique of composition they had skilfully developed, was able to write Sonatas, Symphonies, and String Quartets that 'meant' more than theirs.

Development was rapid. Looking at Beethoven's work alone, if we compare the early piano sonatas or symphonies with the later ones, we see such a progression

22

from the comparatively simple in style and expression to the highly complex that, if we did not know the extra-ordinary speed with which the art of music develops, we might think them to be the work of a century.

It would be a very instructive thing to hear an his-torical programme of keyboard pieces as follows:

An English Elizabethan Pavan and Galliard (late 16th century).

A Purcell Suite (late 17th century).

A Bach Suite (early 18th century).

A Sonata by Haydn or Mozart (later 18th century).

An early Sonata by Beethoven (late 18th century).

A later Sonata by Beethoven (early 19th century).

That programme would include the product of a period of about 250 years, and would give a most in-structive bird's-eye view of the development of one of the greatest art forms, and one of the most magnificent media of human expression that the world has yet seen.

A similar programme of orchestral music would be equally interesting. We possess no orchestral music, strictly speaking, of the sixteenth century, for the or-chestra was then not an organized force, but we could have:

A String Fantasia of Elizabethan days (late 16th century).

A String Fantasia of Purcell (late 17th century).

An Orchestral Suite of Bach (early 18th century).

A Symphony of Haydn or Mozart (late 18th century).

An early Symphony of Beethoven, say his first or second (early 19th century).

A later Symphony of Beethoven, say his fifth, seventh, or ninth.

In hearing such a programme[1] we should be struck with

[1] Both the programmes given are quite possible to any owner of a gramophone who is willing to choose his records on a rational plan.

23

the great development of the Orchestra from Bach to Beethoven. In Bach's day it had no fixed constitution. With Haydn and Mozart it had settled down to a basis of Strings, with two each of Flutes, Oboes (sometimes Clarinets), and Bassoons, Horns and Trumpets, and Kettledrums. With Beethoven we have the same thing enriched, with Clarinets invariable, with greatly improved and consequently more adaptable Brass instruments, and sometimes with Trombones, with all the instruments used more freely and the whole developed into a marvellous means of the expression of the deepest human emotions.

As already stated, with Bach the Harpsichord lingered in the orchestra. From Haydn and Mozart onwards no keyboard instrument is any longer a member of the orchestra (though it may be invited on occasion to play the solo part in Concertos). With them, too, the Harpsichord tends to disappear and to be replaced by the modern Pianoforte (in which the strings are no longer plucked but hammered), and from Beethoven onwards the Pianoforte entirely supersedes the Harpsichord.

Piano and Orchestra are now, we may say, 'ready for anything'—the Piano is ready for Chopin and the orchestra for Wagner, though, as we shall see, he was to develop it, in detail, still further.

KEY DATES

I. ELIZABETHAN COMPOSERS FOR THE KEYBOARD.

(The Virginals, or early Harpsichord.)

Byrd   *c.* 1543–1623.
Bull   *c.* 1562–1628.
Gibbons   1583–1625.

(It will be noted that, roughly speaking, these three composers came into the world at intervals of twenty years, but that they all left the world at about the same time.)

II. THE AGE OF THE SUITE.

Purcell (English)   1658–95.
Bach (German)   1685–1750.
Handel (German; naturalized British)   1685–1759.
D. Scarlatti (Italian)   1685–1757.
Couperin (French)   1668–1733.

(It is very remarkable that Bach, Handel, and Scarlatti should have all been born in the same year—an *Annus Mirabilis.*)

III. THE AGE OF THE SONATA AND SYMPHONY.

Haydn (Austrian)   1732–1809.
Mozart (Austrian)   1756–91.
Beethoven (German)   1770–1827.
Schubert (Austrian)   1797–1828.

(We may call this the Vienna School, as all these composers lived and worked to a greater or less extent in Vienna. Mozart's short life, it will be noticed, fell entirely within the long life of Haydn. Schubert was a quarter of a century younger than Beethoven, but the two died about the same time.)

IV. MUSIC AS ROMANCE

In three chapters there has been hastily sketched the course of twelve centuries' development of music. For the most part the four chapters that remain will be occupied with its further development during a period of little over one century.

This looks all out of balance, and yet it is right. Music during the nineteenth century and the first quarter of the twentieth has become so many-sided (and latterly so experimental) that larger space is needed for its discussion. Moreover, what is near to us in point of time interests us as to details, whereas discussion of what is more remote we are willing to accept in generalized form. The proportions of a concise history of English Literature would probably be roughly the same. I turn to the late Sir Edmund Gosse's *Short History* and find that the period from Chaucer to the coming of Wordsworth occupies 230 pages, and the period from the coming of Wordsworth to the end of 'The Victorian Age' another 160 pages. If Sir Edmund had brought his history down to the present day his proportions would evidently have become very much like mine.

The third chapter closed gloriously with Beethoven—gloriously, since in his work culminated a long development of the resources of the art which had made it a most sensitive instrument for the expression of the sense of beauty and of human emotion. Things sometimes happen very apropos. The period of Beethoven was a period of deepened feeling, and needed such an instrument for its self-expression. Call it, if you like, the age of the French Revolution and of a new social liberty. Or recall how the portraits of Bach, Handel, Haydn, and Mozart show their heads decorously hidden by wigs (except, perhaps, that of Mozart, whose hair is nevertheless powdered and bound with a black ribbon). Then recall the portrait of Beethoven, who wears his own hair (sometimes very ruffled) and, instead of a courtier-like countenance, exhibits in his features determination, independence, and even pugnacity. Rousseau has been at work in the world; thrones are tumbling and thought is free.

And Rousseau has not only overturned an artificial civilization, he has also brought into literature the free spirit of Romance. At all events we usually put this down to Rousseau. He is at least the precursor of the movement, but there follows his name a list of others that takes in, in Germany, Lessing and Schiller and Goethe (for whatever classical leanings these had they exercised a romantic influence also), and Novalis and the Schlegels and Tieck and Hoffmann; in France, Chateaubriand and Lamartine, Victor Hugo and Dumas, George Sand and Flaubert, and many others; and in Britain, Blake and Burns, and Scott and Byron, and Wordsworth and Keats. And there is a parallel movement amongst the painters. We will pick the Frenchmen Delacroix and Géricault as representatives of the early nineteenth-century romantic expression in painting, and, without running round to other countries, leave it at that.

All these men of genius, poets and novelists and dramatists and painters, are imbued with the same overpowering emotion in its different phases—the romantic emotion, a sense of the terror and the beauty of life, and of its pervading mystery. They achieve beauty in their poems and their paintings, but they seek first not so much

27

beauty as the expression of that emotion. Theodore Watts-Dunton has defined the Romantic Movement in literature as 'The Renascence of Wonder'. The term is perhaps wide enough to express all that we want to include. The wide-eyed wonder of the days of Shakespeare and Drake has come to earth again.

Now not only contemporary with these 'Romantic' authors and artists, but also in many cases in intimate personal association with them, we find a group of composers—or, more properly, several such groups. In Germany we have Weber, who has as a personal friend (and often reads) the fantastic Hoffmann, and in his youth has roamed theatrical Germany in the romantic Wilhelm Meister sort of way. And we have Schumann, whose father is a publisher and bookseller, and who, as a boy, has browsed in the parental shop on Moore and Byron, Hoffmann and Jean Paul Richter. And we have Mendelssohn, whose grandfather was one of the early German students of Shakespeare and whose family was closely connected by marriage with that of the brothers Schlegel, Germany's greatest Shakespearians of the period, and the very props and pillars of the German romantic literary movement. And we have Richard Wagner, a keen student of the romantic legends of Northern Europe (but him we will consider in the next chapter).

And in Paris we have Berlioz, a most romantically minded and romantically living individual, who reads Shakespeare and Scott, and Byron and Goethe, and bases his music upon what he reads. And there also we have the Pole, Chopin, consumptive and needing friendship, and finding it in the circle of the romantic novelist, George Sand, and the romantic painter, Delacroix; and the Hungarian Liszt, who frequents the company of

Hugo and Lamartine and George Sand and Delacroix, and has a close intimacy with the romantic novelist 'Daniel Stern', in real life the Countess d'Agoult.

These are the musical Romantics. In their music they seek the same kinds of beauty and express the same kinds of emotion as the poets and novelists and painters with whom they associate or to whose influence they submit. There is as wide a range in their romanticism as there is in that of the literary romanticists. In a Chopin Nocturne you may get the delicate romance of a lyric of Keats; in Berlioz's *Fantastic Symphony* you get the romantic grotesquerie of some parts of Victor Hugo's *Notre Dame*. In Liszt you get the luscious sentiment or gaudy brilliance of certain poems of Byron. In Schumann you get the very German romantic fancy of his favourite Jean Paul. There are many kinds of composer in the Romantic School of Music; yet, different as they are, they stand out, as a body, in strong contrast with the preceding schools, which, vaguely generalizing, we may call the 'Classical'. Wordsworth and Coleridge, and Keats and Shelley, and Blake and Byron have very different styles from one another, and express very different feelings, but they all stand out, both as to style and as to feeling, in strong contrast with, say, Addison or Pope.

Perhaps the distinction between 'Classicism' and 'Romanticism' is one not so much of style as of feeling, but it is both. Put it in this way—that in the music of both Mozart and Schumann you have the expression of a sense both of formal beauty and of emotional beauty, but that in Mozart the balance usually weighs down rather on the side of form and that in Schumann it usually weighs down (and pretty heavily) on the side of emotion.

A word now as to a very definite literary and pictorial

29

influence that comes into music. Some composers actually take a literary scheme, lock, stock, and barrel, and try to reproduce it (or at any rate its series of emotions) in terms of tone. The Symphonies and 'Tone-Poems' of Liszt are a very clear example of that sort of thing. He writes a *Dante Symphony* in three sections, 'Inferno', 'Purgatorio', and 'Magnificat'; or he writes a *Faust Symphony* with sections, 'Faust', 'Margaret', and 'Mephistopheles'; or he writes Tone-Poems, *Mazeppa* (after Byron), and *The Slaughter of the Huns* (after a fresco by Kaulbach at Berlin), and *The Dance of Death* (after Orcagna's famous fresco at Pisa). Sometimes he prefixes to his composition a printed 'programme' of the series of thoughts and imagined sights that have inspired the successive passages of his composition, and so we get the technical term PROGRAMME MUSIC, a term which can be (closely or loosely) applied to a great part of the output of the Romantic School.

But not every composer of that school is 'programmatic', and at the beginning of it we have Beethoven, who has not shaken off his classical sympathies and rarely writes anything we could call 'programme music'; and at the end of it Brahms, who has regained classical sympathies and can perhaps be said to write no 'programme music' at all.

'At the end of it'—those were large words to use. Is the Romantic temper yet banished from music? By no means! Perhaps it never can be banished. Perhaps the art of music is essentially and necessarily a romantic art. Bach was often romantic: so were Byrd and Palestrina. But it was in the first half of the nineteenth century that the great outburst of romantic feeling in all the arts came, and the composers who, at that time, expressed it so plainly and fully in the music we call, for classification's sake, 'The Romantic School'.

In the first chapter of this brief history we analysed music into certain elements—Melody, Harmony, Counterpoint, Form, Orchestration. At any stage of music's development some change takes place in all of these—some change fitting each for its new functions. During the Romantic period there was a considerable development of Orchestration, designed to produce new and vivid colourings fitted for the expression of romantic feeling; Berlioz was a great experimenter in this more varied use of the orchestra, whilst (a similar effort) Liszt, the greatest pianist of the time, invented new pianistic resources. In Form there was the development of the short characteristic piano piece by Schumann and Chopin and others, and of the orchestral Tone-Poem by Liszt. Harmony, under Wagner's hands, became capable of the expression of the minutest shades of feeling—but that belongs to the next chapter.

One special development of the Romantic movement in music must be here passed over in a few words—the expression of national feeling and the use of national folk-rhythms and turns of melody by such ardent patriots as Smetana and Dvořák (Bohemian), Grieg (Norwegian), Glinka, Balakirev, Borodin, Mussorgsky, Rimsky-Korsakov, and Tchaikovsky (Russian), Albeniz, Granados, Turina, and Falla (Spanish). Some of these names bring us down to our own day, when, indeed, the national impulse runs very strongly amongst the composers of many countries, including some of those of our own. Love of one's native land is one of the most strongly romantic inspirations that comes to any of us, and when it came to the musicians it exerted a powerful influence in two ways: it brought into music a new order of feelings, and, by inducing a study of musical folk-expression, it stimulated a greater directness, an 'unsophistication'—a partial abandonment of settled conventions, a breath of fresh air, a wholesome 'Back-to-the-land'.

KEY DATES

Weber (German)	1786–1826.
Berlioz (French)	1803–69.
Mendelssohn (German)	1809–47.
Schumann (German)	1810–56.
Chopin (Polish)	1810–49.
Liszt (Hungarian)	1811–86.
Brahms (German)	1833–97.
Franck (Belgian)	1822–90.

NATIONALISTS

Smetana (Bohemian)	1824–84.
Dvořák (Bohemian)	1841–1904.
Grieg (Norwegian)	1843–1907.
Glinka (Russian)	1804–57.
Balakirev (Russian)	1837–1910.
Mussorgsky (Russian)	1839–81.
Rimsky-Korsakov (Russian)	1844–1908.
Tchaikovsky (Russian)	1840–93.
Albeniz (Spanish)	1860–1909.
Granados (Spanish)	1867–1916.
Falla (Spanish)	1876–1946.
Turina (Spanish)	1882–1949.

V. MUSIC AS DRAMA

THAT people on a stage should sing instead of speak is highly unnatural. So, for that matter, is it unnatural that they should be on a stage at all—a box with three sides and all their speech and action directed to the missing fourth side. So, too, is it highly unnatural that (as in much of Shakespeare, for instance) they should speak in verse. All art is unnatural; all art follows certain conventions—the most 'realistic' drama or picture is no exception from this. A work of art may be defined as the representation of certain facts of nature, first selected (which is already an unnatural process) and then represented in such a way as to draw beauty from some of their features and to enhance that beauty in some way, to the necessary neglect of other features. I have never seen quite this definition before, but it seems to me to meet the case, and to cover all kinds of painting, sculpture, imaginative literature, and, indeed, everything except music, which is, at its best, non-representational, and can only be brought within the definition by very reasonably considering human emotions to be a part of 'nature'.

The combination of drama and music is, then, unnatural. Yet in a way it is natural, *must* be natural, in the sense of meeting a human need, or we should not find it everywhere in the world and in every period of history—in the Greek drama, in the ritual of various religions, in the medieval miracle play, in the Elizabethan Masque, and at last in the Opera, which (as already explained in Chapter II) sprang into existence about the year 1600; it was a result of the classical studies of a little party of learned men and keen musicians in Florence, who thought that in it they were reviving the style and methods of Greek drama.

The first Operas were effective settings of familiar plots from classical mythology, largely in 'recitative'. (Oratorio, which may be loosely defined as non-dramatic opera on sacred subjects, had the same characteristic.) Soon there weakened the rigidity of the recitative convention, the attempt to imitate in song-tone the inflections of speech-tone. Set airs were introduced. By the time of HANDEL the airs had become a very important element—*the* important element. They were of various kinds, and were often difficult. Their very difficulty became a virtue, like the difficulty of an acrobatic feat. To sing them there had come into existence a race of highly trained and highly paid singers, who not only sang airs but *had* airs, a tradition of the operatic stage that persists to the present day, as I feel sure the Musical Director of Covent Garden, London, or the Metropolitan Opera House, New York, could tell us. The display of the infinite capacities of the human voice became the thing, and composers wrote accordingly. Opera had begun in Italy, and most of the famous singers were Italian, and so, in all countries, Opera was sung in Italian. (This also is a tradition that lasted a long time, so that right down to fairly recent years the Covent Garden theatre was officially styled 'The Royal Italian Opera'.)

In the eighteenth century Handel was one great writer of Italian opera. In Handel's time the popular operatic librettist was the Italian Metastasio, who lived in Vienna and wrote innumerable libretti that were set over and over again by innumerable composers, some of them as many as thirty or forty times, so that a regular opera-goer

came to know them as some people know the words of
the English Prayer-book or the Roman Mass.

Reform was needed, for convention had gone too far.
The dramatic element was suffering. GLUCK, in the later
eighteenth century, was the great reformer. He laid
down these principles (and applied them in his later
operas): the music to be a support to the drama; vocal
or other display for the sake of display to be avoided; the
overture to be of such a character as to prepare the mind
of the audience for the play to follow; the orchestration
to be varied according to the degree of interest and passion in the words; too great a disparity between Recita-
tives and Airs to be shunned. Gluck's general aim he
describes as 'a noble simplicity'.

MOZART was forty years Gluck's junior, and had the
advantage of Gluck's example. He attained a great
musical characterization of his *dramatis personae*, yet at
the same time a strong melodic charm. His unerring
sense of musical beauty had full play, yet he was dramatic.
He did not always use the Italian language; for instance,
The Seraglio and *The Magic Flute* had German libretti.
Sometimes (in the traditional German light-opera way)
he used spoken dialogue instead of recitative; at other
times he used recitative, often of that quickly pattered
kind that gets over the ground quickly and is called
recitativo secco, or 'dry recitative'. The plots of the works
of his maturity were drawn from other sources than that
of classical mythology (*Figaro* from Beaumarchais, *Don
Juan* from Spanish legend, and so on). Mozart contri-
buted a good deal towards the demolition of convention.

Then opened the Romantic Period, discussed in the
previous chapter, and with WEBER genuine romantic
opera began. The fairy and magical element, already

c

exploited by Mozart in *The Magic Flute*, was very congenial to him. So was German legend (e.g. in *Der Freischütz*, or 'The Marksman'—an opera about magic bullets and the magic Wolf's Glen, and with a German sentimental love interest). Weber had strong national feeling and used the German language—and in *Oberon* the English. He had the power of awakening romantic feeling with a chord on the strings or with a note on the horn. It has been said that Mendelssohn, in his *Midsummer Night's Dream* Overture, 'first brought the fairies into the orchestra', but Weber, in his *Oberon* Overture, was before him. Weber generally used spoken dialogue in the German national Singspiel ('Song-play' or light opera) style, reserving recitative for important moments before some great air.

At last we come to WAGNER, the German Romantic-Nationalist Opera Composer *par excellence*. His libretti, which he wrote himself, are in the German language and their subjects are usually German legends. He develops a melody of his own, a harmony of his own, a counterpoint of his own (these three very chromatic—i.e. moving much by semitones), and an orchestration of his own. With him all of these things are of such a character as to enable him to express his feelings very minutely yet very musically. For the orchestra he demands enormous resources—a bigger number and variety of instruments than any composer before him. The appalling cost of the present-day concert and opera orchestra is due to Wagner, Berlioz, and twentieth-century War.

In his dramatic aims Wagner is a nineteenth-century Gluck. He wants drama first and music afterwards—or rather he wants a new art which shall merge, on pretty nearly equal terms, the musical art, the poetic-dramatic

36

art, the acting art, the stage-pictorial art. At all events, that is his aim; but, as a matter of fact, the music generally floats uppermost.

As the art of Wagner matures he more and more drops the set divisions into recitative, air, and the like. The larger part of his dialogue is carried by a sort of melodious half-recitative with a pretty elaborate orchestral accompaniment, but in high moments this rises into something more lyrical and approaching in style the older air. To make his medium flexible is one of his cares, and so he invents (or greatly develops) the 'Leading Motive'—a device of attaching to personages, events, or ideas a short scrap of music that expresses them significantly, and that can recur from time to time as those personages, events, or ideas re-enter or as he wishes them to be brought to the mind of the listener. Very much of a Wagner score is made up of these Motives, each treated in very varied ways, yet always retaining its recognizable individuality.

There are weaknesses in Wagner—a certain long-windedness in soliloquy, an attempt at an impossible realism in stage setting, and so on. Yet, take him for all in all, he is a master of masters. His own definition of his achievement would be that he found Opera and left 'Music-Drama' (his own term). Wagner's greatest works are the four dramas of *The Ring of the Nibelung*, *Tristan and Isolde*, *The Mastersingers*, and *Parsifal*. Those represent him at his height. The earlier *Rienzi*, *The Flying Dutchman*, *Lohengrin*, and *Tannhäuser*, however admirable, show him not yet free of the conventional 'operatic' style.

Some other Opera composers must be briefly mentioned. First the Italians. DONIZETTI wrote about seventy operas, typically Italian in their easily flowing tunes and demand for vocal gymnastics. BELLINI did much the same (Chopin greatly loved Bellini's melody and his own is influenced by it). ROSSINI may be roughly classed with Donizetti and Bellini, but he achieved a masterpiece of comedy in *The Barber of Seville* that transcends anything they did. These three were busy in the first third or half of the nineteenth century. With the long-lived VERDI we come almost down to our own day. His earlier works were typically Italian in their facile melody, but in his latest works, *Aïda*, *Othello*, and *Falstaff*, he rose higher—in the last two (which show Wagnerian influence) enormously higher. Puccini was very Italian in his love of the 'popular appeal', but in harmony and orchestration gave his work a clever touch of the modern.

The German MEYERBEER brought out a series of spectacular and glittering works, largely designed to please the Parisian public.

The Frenchman BERLIOZ was very histrionic, and loved the orchestra. He was a typical romantic, and so was alluded to in the last chapter. GOUNOD was more facile. BIZET, in *Carmen*, achieved a masterpiece in the lighter type of work.

STRAUSS has out-Wagnered Wagner in the use of big orchestral battalions; his harmonies are free beyond anything previous. He often revels in horror, as in *Electra* and *Salome*, and sometimes descends to farce, as in the unsatisfactory ending to the bright *Cavalier of the Rose*.

DEBUSSY, in *Pelléas and Mélisande*, has produced a lovely work. Maeterlinck's mysticism and melancholy are reproduced by a directness of method unparalleled in the whole history of opera. There is little attempt at musical beauty as such, though much musical beauty results.

Our own SULLIVAN was a master of light comic opera —of the gay and of the wistful. His French counterpart (from whom he undoubtedly learnt a good deal, despite the denials of the Perfect Sullivanites) was OFFENBACH.

Of Opera composers, as of certain beings mentioned in Scripture, it may be said 'their name is legion'. This chapter merely outlines the course of main events in the development of the operatic art, and readers who want to fill in the outline must do that elsewhere.

KEY DATES

COMPOSERS OF ITALIAN OPERA.

Monteverdi (see Chapter II)	1567–1643.
Handel	1685–1759.
Gluck	1714–87.
Mozart	1756–91.
Rossini	1792–1868.
Donizetti	1797–1848.
Bellini	1801–35.
Verdi	1813–1901.
Puccini	1858–1924.

COMPOSERS OF GERMAN OPERA.

Mozart	1756–95.
Weber	1786–1826.
Wagner	1813–83.
Strauss	1864–1949.

COMPOSERS OF FRENCH OPERA.

Meyerbeer	1791–1864.
Berlioz	1803–69.
Gounod	1818–93.
Offenbach	1819–80.
Bizet	1838–75.
Debussy	1862–1918.

COMPOSERS OF ENGLISH OPERA.

Purcell (see Chapter II)	c. 1658–95.
Sullivan	1842–1900.

VI. IMPRESSIONISM IN MUSIC

AT the end of the nineteenth century there came into music, in a limited yet fairly extensive way, a new style, distinctively French in its origin, which, by analogy with the corresponding movement in French Painting, we call 'Impressionism'. It may be looked upon either as a revolt against Romanticism or as a new mode of Romanticism. Personally I much prefer to call it the latter.

In reading the chapter on 'Music as Romance' it must have occurred to many readers that the early nineteenth century brought into musical activity a new factor—a fertilization of music by contact with literature. We know little of what Bach and Mozart read, and if we did it would not throw a great deal of light upon their music. We do know what Weber and Schumann and Berlioz and Liszt read, and if we did not we should lack something that is very helpful in understanding their music.

Similarly we do not know what pictures Bach and Mozart looked at (if any). But we do know what pictures appealed to Debussy, and with what painters he associated—with what painters and with what poets. And to know this helps greatly to the forming of a clear conception of his aims and musical style.

Debussy was a Frenchman, and the painters and poets who most influenced him were the French poets and painters of his own day and the day before—the Symbolist poets and the Impressionist painters.

The 'Symbolist' Movement in poetry and the 'Impressionist' Movement in painting were at their height when Debussy, returning in 1887 from study in Rome, settled again in Paris. Baudelaire, the chief precursor of

41

the Symbolist Movement, was dead twenty years before, but Verlaine was alive, as also Mallarmé and a group of younger poets who gathered at Mallarmé's house and looked to him as their leader. Debussy frequented this house and imbibed the ideas there current, so it is of interest to us to get as clear an idea as possible of the nature of those ideas.

To describe in a few words the Symbolist Movement in literature is not easy. On its negative side it was a reaction against the big-bow-wow style of the French Romantic poets, and especially of the latest group of them who were known as the 'Parnasseans'. The Symbolists attempted a product altogether more delicate. To an English reader the change of feeling and method from Byron to Rossetti may convey a rough-and-ready idea of the change of feeling from, say, Hugo to Verlaine. And, too, as to 'content', the comparison between Ruskin and Pater may help. Ruskin was the apostle of what has been called 'moralized beauty'—a sort of preacher-statesman-critic. Pater was aesthetic and a frank hedonist—not the fruit of experience, but experience itself is the end. 'A counted number of pulses only is given to us of a variegated and dramatic life. How may we see in them all that is to be seen in them by the finest senses?'[1]

There was, then, a good deal of the sensuous and the voluptuous about the Symbolist group, but it was a delicate sensuousness and a refined voluptuousness, expressed with an aristocratic grace.

[1] From the conclusion of Pater's *Renaissance*. He omitted it from the second and third editions, as he 'conceived that it might possibly corrupt some young men into whose hands it might fall'. In the fourth edition, somehow reassured, he restored it.

Nothing was coarsely or bluntly expressed. Indeed, what a poem said was almost less important than what the reader was led to think between the lines. There was a constant stimulus to the imagination, and there comes in the force of the title the Movement adopted. Words were used as symbols. They suggested rather than expressed.

This often led to obscurity, and in some cases obscurity actually seemed to be the object. Until lately nobody has ever attempted to translate into plain English Mallarmé's *L'après-midi d'un faune*, and probably nobody will succeed either in translating it really adequately into any language or in rendering a satisfactory prose paraphrase. But Debussy has, so to speak, 'translated' it into music, and as music *The Afternoon of a Faun* gives frequent delight to thousands of listeners.

Poetry like Mallarmé's approaches the quality of music. More than any other art, music (at its best) is the art of the subconscious.

The reader who is pretty well acquainted with even three or four of Debussy's compositions, but has not previously grasped the connexion between his style and the aims of the Symbolist poets, must surely now see a little light. The Symbolists were attempting a poetry like music, and Debussy, inspired by them, attempted a music more musical than had previously (or, at any rate, recently) been written, in that it eschewed, as far as possible, those Beethoven-like or Wagner-like complexities of development of theme which resemble argument or rhetoric, those Lisztian emotional passages that can easily be re-expressed in words, and (usually) those 'programmatic' attempts at description of action which belong most properly to the short story or novel.

43

So much for the Poet-Symbolists; now as to the Painter-Impressionists, a closely allied group. Their aims differed from those of the Symbolists, one may say, merely as the art of painting differs from the art of poetry. Sir Edmund Gosse has said of the Symbolist poets that their verse was 'a murmur of waters flowing under a veil of rushes', and we may say of the Impressionist artists that their painting was a play of light. Like the poets, they shunned drama ('Light is the chief personage in a picture' was one of Manet's maxims), 'literary' subjects, classical formality, and all established conventions, and sought to make out of the representation of effects of luminosity a kind of beautifully painted music. A technical procedure which is of interest, because in a moment we shall find a slight musical analogy to it, is the process of painting in pure, unmixed colours in such a close juxtaposition that at the proper distance the eye sees them merged into their intended composite. Like the poets, they tried to achieve delicacy of nuance; as an example, they discovered that shadows are not necessarily black, but have their varying colours.

Manet may be considered the founder of the School, other members being Monet, Degas, Renoir, Pissarro, and Cézanne.

The comparison between the Impressionist painting and Debussy's music is quickly made. Debussy, too, as has already been said, avoided the dramatic, the narrative, the formal, the conventional, the involved. The preoccupation of the Impressionist painters with light *qua* light had its parallel, with this Impressionist musician, in a preoccupation with tone *qua* tone.

To take an example, frequently his chords are separate entities, their notes chosen and spaced on the piano (or distributed in the orchestra) in such a way as to produce the desired momentary tonal effect, and with little or no regard to their neighbours in such matters as the 'preparation' or 'resolution' of discords. This is a technicality, but some readers will have enough knowledge of harmony to grasp it.

For the most part the harmony of Strauss is an extension of that of Wagner, whose harmony is an extension of that of Beethoven, whose harmony is an extension of that of Haydn. But Debussy's harmonies very frequently indeed can be derived from nothing heard in previous composers. Gifted with a very keen ear, he had listened to bugles and particularly bells, and had studied the 'overtones', the combination of which we wrongly term a single note—those overtones the particular character and relative strengths of which, in any particular performance of a note, give that note its 'timbre'. And often he reinforced some of those overtones by the addition of actual notes, and so arrived at tonal effects by a synthetic process somewhat similar to the technical process of the Impressionist painters above referred to.

Like the Poet-Symbolists and the Painter-Impressionists, Debussy is generally very 'atmospheric', and so, like them, he has been charged with vagueness. There is abundant design in a picture of Monet or a composition of Debussy, but (to quote *The Times* obituary notice of Monet in 1926, for the sake of its interesting allusion to Debussy):

'It stands to reason that if an artist is designing in atmospheric values, in veils of light, the design will not be so emphatic, so easily grasped as if he were designing in solid forms, but nobody can look with attention at a picture by Monet and regard it as a mere representation of

45

the facts and conditions. In this respect his work might well be compared to the music of his countryman, Claude Debussy, in which under an atmospheric shimmer, the melodies are not so immediately recognizable as they are in the works of Bach and Beethoven, but are nevertheless present to an attentive ear.'

Debussy and Ravel are both 'Impressionists', but Ravel is less truly so than Debussy, inasmuch as his music is less 'misty' or 'atmospheric'. Put Franck and his pupil d'Indy on one side and Debussy and Ravel on the other and you seem to have just two styles; then take Franck and d'Indy out of the discussion altogether, and look only at Debussy and Ravel, and *their* distinction of style becomes clear enough. (Put red on one side and various blues on the other and you have an evident contrast; put red out of sight and your various shades of blue begin to sort themselves into classifications of their own.)

Comparing any sufficiently large body of mature work of the two composers, it will be realized that Debussy's is more 'fluid' and Ravel's somewhat more 'solid', i.e. more firm and clear in its outlines. Or Debussy's work is rather more 'subjective' and Ravel's more 'objective'. Partly this is due to differences of harmonic idiom. A good way of realizing the difference would be to hear, on consecutive evenings, Debussy's Opera, *Pelléas and Mélisande*, and Ravel's Opera, *L'Heure Espagnole*. It would then be found that Debussy was much more occupied in evoking emotional 'atmosphere', and Ravel in musically characterizing the sense of words which expressed clear thoughts or described dramatic 'events'. To this the rejoinder may be made that the literary subjects are very different and call for widely differing treatment, but to that may be re-rejoined that nobody imposed these

46

subjects upon the respective composers, and that their very choice of them emphasizes the psychological difference between the two men.

The Italian composer, Casella, has drawn a fairly apt parallel by suggesting that as Schumann stands to Mendelssohn in German Romanticism, so does Debussy stand to Ravel in French Impressionism.

Debussy and Ravel are to be looked upon as the leading composers of the 'school' now under discussion, but, in a greater or lesser way, many other composers have submitted to the 'Impressionist' influence. To take an example from British music—it is impossible to hear, one after the other, three or four of the delicate piano pieces of John Ireland without realizing that, consciously or unconsciously, he is, in part, an 'Impressionist'. There is, too, a good deal of Impressionist influence in some of the work of Delius. So there is in the work of Loeffler. And so one might go on. Pure musical Impressionism is now perhaps a waning force, but it is a force nevertheless. The Italian composer, Respighi, alluded to Debussy as follows: 'The spirit, the aesthetics, and the technique of modern music were not established in a precise, lasting, and definite manner until the appearance of the orchestral *Nocturnes*, *The Afternoon of a Faun*, and *Pelléas and Mélisande*. . . . Debussy's work represents the greatest revolution in modern musical art.'

KEY DATES

Debussy   1862–1918.
Ravel   1875–1937.

VII. THE MUSIC OF TO-DAY

THE most difficult and thankless task that any writer on music can undertake is to attempt to classify the composers contemporary with himself. They are so many, and Time, the great critic, has not yet weeded. They are so various, and 'one man in his time plays many parts', changing greatly in behaviour as he marches forward from youth to old age. The critic brings his microscope to bear upon a group of composers and, lo! the microscope has turned into a kaleidoscope with a series of images ever changing in relative position and in colour.

The handiest simple division, it seems to me, is into two groups—the New Romantics and the Anti-Romantics. But it must be clearly understood that this division is not absolute, and that some composers have produced works that would entitle them to consideration under both heads. At all events, the very headings of this division (whichever composers we may decide to bring under each heading) make it clear that there are two main trends in music to-day—the trend of those who are carried along by the Romantic impulse of the last century, and the trend of those who resist that impulse and are, indeed, many of them in active revolt against it.

STRAUSS I look upon as certainly a Newer Romantic. In his work (his Tone-Poems and his Operas) he 'produced' the line of that of Liszt and Wagner. Wagner took the harmony and orchestration of Beethoven and introduced new subtleties into it, and Strauss took the harmony and orchestration of Wagner and gradually subtilized it still farther. The feeling of all Strauss has written is definitely romantic. Elgar, too, with his 'noble' musical themes and his mysticism and his warm, rich orchestration, I look upon as a Newer Romantic, and one of the worthiest. Holst and Vaughan Williams are in the main romantic, though in some of their works they adopt a style approaching that of the Anti-Romantics : the same may be said of Walton and most of the younger British, American, Russian, and other composers. Macdowell, the American, was decidedly a Romantic—almost a German Romantic of the original kind.

The feeling of all that SCRIABIN wrote is romantic: he evolved, step by step, a system of harmony and melody, and even orchestration, peculiar to himself, but, whether in his earlier piano works he is emulating the grace of Chopin, or in his later piano and orchestral works trying to express the emotion of his own particular brand of theosophical thought, he is always intensely romantic.

SCHÖNBERG, too, is, it seems to me, a Newer Romantic. His early string sextet, *Resplendent Night* ('Verklärte Nacht') and his *Songs of Gurra* ('Gurrelieder'), whatever traces of his own personality they may show, are quite in the Wagner tradition.

In his latest works Schönberg used a harmony (or a deliberate dis-harmony) so novel, and to less tolerant ears so excruciating, that the essential romanticism of his feeling may escape many listeners. But he is, I think, generally or always romantic in feeling, and certainly the literary texts he sets are such. The romanticism of both texts and music is, to my mind, often over-ripe (not to use a stronger word), and to me Schönberg lies under the suspicion of being a romantic decadent—but that is a personal view, and not to be dogmatically imposed on my readers, but only to be gently suggested for their consideration. Sometimes, latterly, Schönberg, who in

49

his earlier orchestral works called for immense instrumental resources, thinned down his requirements to a few instruments, producing a few mere lines of contrastingly coloured tone; in this he resembles the Anti-Romantics now to be discussed, but in feeling I think him to be definitely a romantic.

Stravinsky and Bartók I look upon as the two typical Anti-Romantics. STRAVINSKY in his earlier settings of the Diaghilev Russian Ballets accepted very romantic subjects (*The Firebird*, *Petrouchka*, &c.), but his treatment always showed at least a tendency away from the 'subjective' and towards the 'objective'. Many foolish things have been said about Stravinsky's 'objectivity' in such works as *The Rite of Spring* ('Le Sacre du Printemps'), and some other works, which have been claimed as symphonic in intention when all the time they are obviously closely detailed settings of a ballet 'programme'. Nevertheless Stravinsky veers strongly in the anti-Romantic direction, and now that he is devoting himself less to the provision of ballet scores and more to 'absolute music' (the Piano Concerto and the Piano Sonata are examples) this will be the more easily seen. In these works he is deliberately seeking a new 'classicism'. Many listeners in hearing them must have recognized a great deal of Bach influence. The harmony is not by any means always such as Bach would have approved in the work of one of his pupils, and as for the counterpoint, just as a well-schooled lawyer can often 'drive a coach and four through an Act of Parliament', so Stravinsky can produce something that to a casual glance of the eye looks like the authentic Bach-period weaving of melodies, yet to the ear sounds like something a good deal more pungent. There is, however, no saying where Stravinsky will end.

He actually now often closes his pieces with plain simple chords such as any village schoolmistress could play on her harmonium—the common chord, C-E-G, is not disdained.

Both Schönberg and Stravinsky have been fond of theorizing, but, as it seems to me, Schönberg often theorized before he started and then worked to a theory, whilst Stravinsky, who to hear him talk does the same thing, in reality usually works under a subconscious impulse, in however experimental a mood he may be, and then theorizes afterwards—the safer plan. (But this is not always true of him.)

The much-reviled, yet essentially gentle, Bartók is, for my purposes of rough classification, to be placed beside Stravinsky. He sought to cast off the romantic clothing of the nineteenth century, and when in a radio programme he suddenly appeared naked and unashamed, no wonder that some listeners put their hands to their eyes and cried 'Fie!'

What will come of all these experiments? Nobody can say. It may be that to-day's experimenters will be forgotten save by the erudite writers and conscientious readers of twenty-first-century works on the history of music. Yet if this happens, perhaps the world will be none the less indebted; for the work of the Anti-Romantics of to-day may be a foundation which is to lie underground yet to support a brave structure.

Certain it is that the romantic style often seems near exhaustion. Can anything valuable now be done in that style or shall we make a clean start, as, at the beginning of the seventeenth century, the Florentine band of experimenters (see Chapter II), realizing, more or less consciously, that the unaccompanied choral style of

51

Palestrina and Byrd was nearing exhaustion, turned to something else—something which at first must to many listeners have seemed crude and paltry as compared with the glories of what it was trying to supersede, yet which proved to be the basis of all the music of the following three centuries.

The present is certainly an age of experiment. Men are experimenting in the combination of keys, and in the introduction of quarter-tones and third-tones and even of twelfth-tones. They are experimenting in orchestral 'colour'. They are trying new devices in Melody, Harmony, Counterpoint, Form—in all the 'elements' of music outlined in my first chapter. Schönberg and others have used the 'Dodecuple Scale' (with its twelve notes of the octave all treated as of equal status) and a very arbitrary process in the arrangement of those notes, known as the 'Note Row' (or 'Tone Row').

To me some of the experiments are mad, and when we think so we must say so. But we must say so with this admission—that the keenest music-lovers of the past have often used that word 'mad' about music that is now welcomed by every listener, simple or learned.

'The real purpose of history', began the first chapter of this booklet, 'is to explain the present, to show how we and our ways came about, and thus partially to interpret us to ourselves.' On reflection that is only part of the purpose of history, and another part is to help us to bear tolerantly what the future may bring. The eye that can look back to the one distant horizon can look forward to the other. Man's journey hither has been one of effort and trial, but has been worth it all; his journey hence will also be one of effort and trial, yet, emboldened by retrospect, we may hope that it, too, will bring a reward.

The great need of the moment is patience. If we cannot always applaud these vigorous runners, let us at least not obstruct them.

KEY DATES

Elgar (English)	1857–1934
Macdowell (American)	1861–1908
Strauss (German)	1864–1949
Scriabin (Russian)	1872–1915
Schönberg (Austrian)	1874–1951
Bartók (Hungarian)	1881–1945
Stravinsky (Russian)	1882–1971

(The above are arranged in order of birth.)